3RD GRADE HISTORY: THE EGYPTIAN CIVILIZATION

SPEEDY
PUBLISHING

Speedy Publishing LLC
40 E. Main St. #1156
Newark, DE 19711
www.speedypublishing.com

Ancient Egypt was a civilization of ancient Northeastern Africa, concentrated along the lower reaches of the Nile River in what is now the modern country of Egypt.

Ancient Egypt was one of the earliest in world history. Ancient Egypt was one of the greatest and most powerful civilizations in the history.

The first Pharaoh of Egypt, Menes, united the Upper and Lower parts of Egypt into a single civilization.

Ancient Egypt was grouped into three major kingdoms called the Old Kingdom, the Middle Kingdom, and the New Kingdom.

The Old Kingdom lasted from 2575 BC to 2150 BC. The Old Kingdom is most famous as a time when many pyramids were built.

The Middle Kingdom lasted from 1975 BC to 1640 BC. During this time all of Egypt was united under a single government and Pharaoh.

The New Kingdom lasted from around 1520 BC to 1075 BC. The New Kingdom was the golden age of the civilization of Ancient Egypt.

One of the
most important
inventions of
the Ancient
Egyptians
was writing.

53589880R00020

Made in the USA
San Bernardino, CA
21 September 2017